THE ULTIMATE
JACKSONVILLE JAGUARS
TRIVIA BOOK

A Collection of Amazing Trivia Quizzes
and Fun Facts for Die-Hard Jags Fans!

Ray Walker

To my CJO

The best

12/10/21

Exclusive Free Book
Crazy Sports Stories

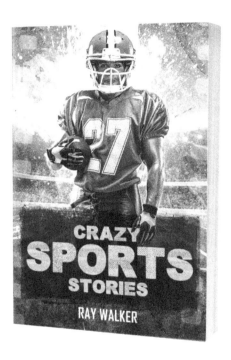

As a thank you for getting a copy of this book I would like to offer you a free copy of my book Crazy Sports Stories which comes packed with interesting stories from your favorite sports such as Football, Hockey, Baseball, Basketball and more.

Grab your free copy over at
RayWalkerMedia.com/Bonus

CONTENTS

INTRODUCTION

Team fandom should be inspirational. Our attachment to our favorite teams should fill us with pride, excitement, loyalty, and a sense of fulfillment in knowing that we are part of a community with many other fans who feel the same way.

Jacksonville Jaguars fans are no exception. Within their short, developing history in the NFL, the Jaguars have inspired their supporters to strive for greatness with their tradition of colorful players, memorable eras, big moves, and unique moments.

This book is meant to be a celebration of those moments, and an examination of the collection of interesting, impressive, or important details that allow us to understand the full stories behind the players and the team.

You may use the book as you wish. Each chapter contains twenty quiz questions in a mixture of multiple choice/true or false formats, an answer key (don't worry, it's on a separate page!), and a section of ten "Did You Know" factoids about the team.

Some will use it to test themselves with the quiz questions. How much Jaguars history did you really know? How many of the finer points can you remember? Some will use it competitively (isn't that the heart of sports?), waging contests with friends and fellow devotees to see who can lay claim to being the biggest fan. Some will enjoy it as a learning experience, gaining insight to enrich their fandom and add color to their understanding of their favorite team. Still others may use it to teach, sharing the wonderful anecdotes inside to inspire a new generation of fans to hop aboard the Jaguars bandwagon.

Whatever your purpose may be, we hope you enjoy delving into the amazing background of Jacksonville Jaguars football!

Oh … and for the record, information and statistics in this book are current up to the beginning of 2021. The Jaguars will surely topple more records and win more awards as the seasons pass, so keep this in mind when you're watching the next game with your friends, and someone starts a conversation with "Did you know…"

CHAPTER 1:

ORIGINS & HISTORY

QUIZ TIME!

1. In which year did the Jaguars begin playing in the National Football League?

   a. 1991

   b. 1995

   c. 1997

   d. 2000

2. The franchise was nearly called the Jacksonville Gators, partially to because of the tie in with the very popular University of Florida among local fans, partially because of the abundance of alligators in the region, and partially to honor a defunct rugby team from the city by that name.

   a. True

   b. False

3. How was the nickname "Jaguars" chosen for the team?

   a. The owner named the team after the luxury car company Jaguar, because the city of Jacksonville had been criticized as neither large nor rich enough to support an NFL team. "Jaguars" was thus intended to add a touch of class to the organization

b. "Jaguars" was the winner chosen in a local fan contest. It was entered because the Jacksonville Zoo owned the oldest jaguar in North America, and edged out "Stingrays" and "Sharks" for the win

c. The team founder wanted an alliterative name and initially chose "Jacksonville Jungle Cats." However, owners of the Detroit Lions, Cincinnati Bengals, and Carolina Panthers protested that the name infringed on theirs, so the team settled on "Jaguars" as a compromise

d. "Jaguars" was the name suggested by the 5-year-old son of the team owner, who had been allowed (within reason) by his father to select the club's new nickname

4. How many home stadiums have the Jaguars used in Jacksonville during their first twenty years as an NFL franchise?

   a. One stadium
   b. Two stadiums
   c. Three stadiums
   d. Four stadiums

5. Who was the founder of the Jacksonville Jaguars?

   a. Shahid Khan
   b. Wayne Huizenga
   c. Eddie DeBartolo Jr.
   d. Wayne Weaver

6. In which season did the Jaguars earn their first ever playoff berth?

    a. 1995
    b. 1996
    c. 1999
    d. 2007

7. The Jacksonville Jaguars won more games than any other NFL team during the period between 1995 - 2005.

    a. True
    b. False

8. How many times in their franchise history have the Jaguars won a division title?

    a. The Jaguars have never won a division title
    b. One time
    c. Three times
    d. Six times

9. Which two players were the first Jaguars ever to be named to the NFL All-Pro First Team?

    a. Left tackle Tony Boselli and punter Brian Barker
    b. Wide receiver Jimmy Smith and right tackle Leon Searcy
    c. Defensive end Tony Brackens and quarterback Mark Brunell
    d. Linebacker Kevin Hardy and safety Carnell Lake

10. Where do the Jacksonville Jaguars rank among NFL franchises when it comes to most Super Bowls won?

a. 8th overall

b. Tied for 16th overall

c. 20th overall

d. Tied for last overall

11. How did the Jaguars fare during their 20th anniversary season in the NFL?

a. Missed the playoffs

b. Lost in the wild card playoffs to the New England Patriots

c. Lost in the divisional playoffs to the New England Patriots

d. Lost in the AFC championship to the New England Patriots

12. The longest stretch the Jaguars have gone without making the playoffs is nine years between 2008-2016.

a. True

b. False

13. Which team did Jacksonville face in its first ever NFL game (which resulted in a 10 – 3 loss)?

a. Miami Dolphins

b. New York Jets

c. Houston Oilers

d. Green Bay Packers

14. What were the details surrounding the Jaguars' first ever shutout in the NFL?

a. It was a 20-0 win over the Tampa Bay Buccaneers in 1996
b. It was a 14-0 loss to the Indianapolis Colts in 1995
c. It was a 17-0 win over the Cleveland Browns in 1997
d. It was a 44-0 loss to the Detroit Lions in 1995

15. Which player kicked the first ever field goal for the Jacksonville Jaguars?

a. Mike Hollis
b. Josh Scobee
c. Jaret Holmes
d. Seth Marler

16. As of 2021, Jacksonville is tied with the Pittsburgh Steelers and the New England Patriots as the franchises that have sent more players to the Pro Bowl than any other NFL franchise.

a. True
b. False

17. How did Jacksonville fare in its first ever NFL playoff run?

a. Lost in the wild card playoffs to the Buffalo Bills
b. Lost in the divisional playoffs to the Denver Broncos
c. Lost in the divisional playoffs to the New York Jets
d. Lost in the AFC championship to the New England Patriots

18. What is Jacksonville's franchise record for most victories recorded by the club in a single regular season?

a. 10 wins

b. 11 wins

c. 12 wins

d. 14 wins

19. What is the name of the Jaguars' mascot?

a. Jerry the Jaguar

b. Jagged

c. Jaxson de Ville

d. The Jaguars do not have a team mascot

20. The Jacksonville football franchise has, at some point, been included in both the AFC Central and AFC South divisions.

a. True

b. False

QUIZ ANSWERS

1. B – 1995

2. B – False

3. B – "Jaguars" was the winner chosen in a local fan contest. It was entered because the Jacksonville Zoo owned the oldest jaguar in North America, and edged out "Stingrays" and "Sharks" for the win

4. A – One stadium

5. D – Wayne Weaver

6. B – 1996

7. B – False

8. C – Three times

9. A – Left tackle Tony Boselli and punter Brian Barker

10. D – Tied for last overall

11. A – Missed the playoffs

12. A – True

13. C – Houston Oilers

14. D – It was a 44-0 loss to the Detroit Lions in 1995

15. A – Mike Hollis

16. B – False

17. D – Lost in the AFC championship to the New England Patriots

18. D – 14 wins

19. C – Jaxson de Ville

20. A – True

DID YOU KNOW?

1. For seven consecutive years, from 2013-2019, the Jaguars were a designated home team for a game in London. These games have been played at Wembley Stadium, and despite being paused due to the global pandemic in 2020, the team is scheduled to resume playing in London again during the 2021 season.

2. Jacksonville had been home to professional footballs team before the Jaguars arrived. The Jacksonville Sharks played in the World Football League in 1974 but ceased operations that same year due to financial difficulties. The Jacksonville Express took their spot in the league in 1975, but the entire WFL folded during that same season.

3. TIAA Bank Stadium, the current home of the Jaguars, opened in 1995 and has cycled through three previous names: Jacksonville Municipal Stadium, AllTel Stadium and EverBank Field.

4. While the Jaguars are an anchor tenant of TIAA Bank Stadium, it is not their home exclusively. The stadium annually hosts the Gator Bowl and has also been used for the Super Bowl, the U.S. men's national soccer team, the Jacksonville Armada of the NASL and many musical acts to perform.

5. As a new team entering the NFL in 1995, the Jaguars paid a $140 million franchise fee for the right to join the league.

For context, when the Houston Texans joined in 2002, they paid an expansion fee of $700 million.

6. The first touchdown in Jaguars history was an exciting one. On September 10, 1995, with Jacksonville facing the Cincinnati Bengals, quarterback Steve Beuerlein found running back Randy Jordan for a 71-yard scoring pass that gave the Jags their first ever lead in an NFL game.

7. Jacksonville's biggest NFL rival is generally thought to be the Tennessee Titans. The two teams share a division, and the rivalry was at its most heated in 1999, when the Jaguars went 14-2, but both losses came to the Titans, who then also knocked Jacksonville out of the playoffs. The Titans have the advantage in the head-to-head rivalry with a 32-21 head-to-head record.

8. The Jaguars rivalry with the Titans has often gotten personal. In one season, the Jags charged that Gregg Williams, the Titans' defensive coordinator, stole Jacksonville's playbook. Titans coach Jeff Fisher stoked the flames by calling Jacksonville's stadium the Titans' "second home field." Even fans got into the act, referring to each other's teams as "The Flaming Thumbtacks" and "The Glitter Kitties," respectively.

9. Jacksonville's franchise low point for fewest victories recorded by the club in a single regular season is just one, which they set during the 2020 season

10. In the beginning, the Jaguars were surprisingly competitive for an expansion team. Though they missed the playoffs in

their first season, they made the playoff for the next four years, even winning a handful of playoff games to advance during those seasons.

CHAPTER 2:

JERSEYS & NUMBERS

QUIZ TIME!

1. When they began playing in the NFL in 1995, the Jaguars used what color scheme for their home and away uniforms?

    a. Purple, yellow and white
    b. Navy blue, gold and white
    c. Teal, black, white and gold
    d. Teal, silver and black

2. The numbers 0 and 00 have been banned from circulation by Jacksonville's ownership, as they are seen to represent a losing attitude.

    a. True
    b. False

3. How many stripes run from the crown to the back of the neck on the current version of the Jaguars helmets?

    a. Zero stripes
    b. One gold stripe

c. Two teal stripes

d. Two gold stripes and one white stripe

4. Which four-time Pro Bowl running back finished his career wearing number 31 for Jacksonville, though he played only sparingly in two games for the Jaguars?

a. Priest Holmes

b. Terrell Davis

c. Shaun Alexander

d. Jamaal Charles

5. How many outlines in different colors surrounded the numbers on the inaugural Jacksonville Jaguars jerseys in 1995?

a. No outlines

b. One outline - gold

c. Two outlines - gold and black

d. Three outlines - gold, white and black

6. Which jersey number has proven to be most popular with Jaguars fans in 2021, having sold the most Jacksonville jerseys on NFL.com?

a. Quarterback Trevor Lawrence's number 16

b. Tight end Tim Tebow's number 85

c. Wide receiver D.J. Chark's number 17

d. Running back Travis Etienne's number 1

7. The white jerseys worn by Jacksonville are often said to have been "jinxed" and therefore the team avoids wearing them whenever the choice is theirs.

a. True

b. False

8. Who is the defensive lineman to wear the highest numbered jersey (number 99) for the most games in Jaguars franchise history?

a. Marcell Dareus

b. Sen'Derrick Marks

c. Marcus Stroud

d. Joel Smeenge

9. The current version of the Jaguars uniform includes four colors. Which of the following is NOT used as a primary color for the pants in any of their uniform combinations?

a. Gold

b. Black

c. Teal

d. White

10. Which Jaguar agreed to give up his number 16 to wide receiver Denard Robinson, without asking for anything in return, so that Robinson could wear the same digits he had in high school and college?

a. Taylor Price

b. Ace Sanders

c. Jordan Shipley

d. Cecil Shorts

11. Five players have worn number 10 for the Jaguars. Which of these players scored the most career points?

a. Quarterback Jamie Martin

b. Wide receiver Donte Moncrief

c. Wide receiver Laviska Shenault Jr.

d. Kicker Josh Scobee

12. Quarterback Mark Brunell is the only Jaguar to have ever worn the number 8 on his jersey.

a. True

b. False

13. Why did star running back Maurice Jones-Drew choose to wear number 32 on the back of his jersey for Jacksonville?

a. Because he idolized Hall of Fame running back Marcus Allen, who also wore number 32

b. Because the running back LaDainian Tomlinson had set the NFL single season touchdown record at 31, and Jones-Drew wanted to break that record

c. Because he was not drafted until the second round, meaning that 32 NFL teams had passed on him in the first round

d. Because he wanted to honor his three older sisters and two older brothers in a meaningful way for their support of him growing up

14. How many jersey numbers have the Jacksonville Jaguars retired for their former players?

a. Zero jersey numbers

b. Two jersey numbers

c. Four jersey numbers

d. Five jersey numbers

15. Which defensive end wore number 90 for his entire eight-year Jacksonville career?

    a. Renaldo Wynn
    b. Yannick Ngakoue
    c. Chris Smith
    d. Tony Brackens

16. Eight players have worn the number 1 for Jacksonville, and every single one of them was a quarterback.

    a. True
    b. False

17. Lucky number 7 has been worn by six Jaguars players over the years. Which athlete wore it for the longest amount of time?

    a. Quarterback Byron Leftwich
    b. Kicker Richie Cunningham
    c. Quarterback Chad Henne
    d. Kicker Aldrick Rosas

18. After offensive lineman Eugene Chung wore number 69 for Jacksonville in their inaugural 1995 season, how many years went by before anyone wore the number again?

    a. Three years
    b. Five years
    c. Ten years
    d. No one else has worn that number for the Jaguars yet

19. Which number did star offensive tackle Tony Boselli, who was named to the Pro Bowl five times, wear on the back of his jersey for Jacksonville?

a. Number 71

b. Number 75

c. Number 77

d. Number 79

20. The Jaguars have retired more jersey numbers than any other NFL franchise has.

   a. True

   b. False

QUIZ ANSWERS

1. C – Teal, black, white, and gold

2. B – False

3. A – Zero stripes

4. D – Jamaal Charles

5. C – Two outlines - gold and black

6. B – Tight end Tim Tebow's number 85

7. B – False

8. C – Marcus Stroud

9. A – Gold

10. C – Jordan Shipley

11. D – Kicker Josh Scobee

12. A – True

13. C – Because he was not drafted until the second round, meaning that 32 NFL teams had passed on him in the first round

14. A – Zero jersey numbers

15. D – Tony Brackens

16. B – False

17. C – Quarterback Chad Henne

18. B – Five years

19. A – Number 71

20. B – False

DID YOU KNOW?

1. The original Jaguars logo proposed by the club met with resistance from Ford Motor Company, who felt that it was too similar to the logo used for their Jaguar brand vehicles. The two parties worked it out in a friendly manner that resulted in a changed logo by the club and a sponsorship by the automaker.

2. When the Jacksonville Jaguars and Carolina Panthers entered the NFL together in 1995, both used teal in their color scheme. Jaguars owner Wayne Weaver explained that the teal tongue in Jacksonville's logo was a result of "feeding Panthers to our Jaguars."

3. Because they play in subtropical climate, the Jaguars almost always choose to wear their white uniforms during home games in the warm weather months of the season. This allows them to stay cool while forcing their opponents to play in darker colors that absorb the heat, theoretically giving Jacksonville an advantage.

4. In 2013, the team officially used of the commonly-used "Jags" nickname in one of the team's logos for the first time. This was placed on a shield design as the team's secondary mark after new owner Shahid Khan requested a redesign for the franchise.

5. Thus far in their history, the Jaguars have worn an anniversary patch in 2004, 2014 and 2019, celebrating the team's 10th, 20th and 25th anniversaries, respectively.

6. Some have described the Jaguars' all gold "Color Rush" uniforms as one of the worst designs in NFL history, and the team is often criticized for looking like mustard when they wear them. Even Jacksonville quarterback Blake Bortles admitted he was not a fan, saying "I think somebody's got to tell the truth … I think they're ugly as hell."

7. Superstition may have scared some Jaguars away from wearing the number 13. Only five players in franchise history have chosen it for themselves, and none wore it at all until wide receiver Quan Cosby tried it in 2012. Though it was likely a coincidence, his NFL career ended after that season.

8. Since 1973, the NFL no longer allows players to wear jersey number 0 or 00. Though some franchises issued the number prior to this, no Jacksonville Jaguar will ever wear these digits.

9. The lowest number that Jacksonville has unofficially retired by inducting it into the Pride of the Jaguars is 8, worn by iconic franchise quarterback Mark Brunell.

10. The highest number that Jacksonville has unofficially retired by inducting it into the Pride of the Jaguars is 82, worn by productive wide receiver Jimmy Smith.

CHAPTER 3:

CATCHY NICKNAMES

QUIZ TIME!

1. By which franchise nickname are the Jaguars most commonly referred to?

    a. The Cats
    b. The J's
    c. Jax Town
    d. The Jags

2. Jaguars quarterback Blake Bortles often referred to his throwing lanes as "Bortles' Portals" when discussing route trees with his wide receivers and tight ends during positional meetings.

    a. True
    b. False

3. The longtime home of the Jaguars, TIAA Bank Stadium, once offered all of the following sections from which fans can watch a game, except for which one?

    a. FanDuelville
    b. Family Ville

c. The Sky Patio

d. The Bud Light Party Zone

4. Which Jaguars player was known to fans and teammates by the nickname "Big Game," thanks to his performance in high pressure situations during key college games and the Super Bowl?

a. Cornerback Jalen Ramsey

b. Quarterback Mark Brunell

c. Wide receiver Torry Holt

d. Kicker Josh Scobee

5. How did Jaguars linebacker Myles Jack become known around the league as "Click Clack Jack"?

a. He gave himself the nickname as a handle on the social media platform Twitter

b. He loved to run up and down the stadium stairways in his cleats to train, and teammates noticed the distinctive noise

c. He would chastise opposing players who he'd tackled by making a loud clicking sound with his mouth

d. Coaches would frequently catch him clicking buttons on his cell phone during meetings

6. Which unflattering nickname was Jaguars running back Fred Taylor given due to his tendency to suffer injuries?

a. Fragile Fred

b. Training Room Taylor

c. Mr. IR

d. Freddie Fracture

7. Jacksonville strong safety Donovan Darius was known as "Hooters" because his initials formed "Double D"; a term of measurement that indicates very large sized breasts.

   a. True
   b. False

8. Why was Jaguars quarterback Nick Foles given the nickname "Big Dick Nick" by former teammate Connor Barwin?

   a. Because, according to Barwin, Foles refused to ever pick up the check when members of the team went out to dinner together
   b. Because Barwin was impressed by Foles's performance under pressure during the fourth quarter of a close playoff game
   c. Because Foles was fearless and never hesitated when approaching single women to ask for a date or a phone number
   d. Because Barwin mentioned Foles in response to an internet question about which football player had the largest genitalia

9. Jaguars kicker Stephen Hauschka was dubbed what after converting many field goals in key situations?

   a. Mr. Clutch
   b. Stevie Cool
   c. Hausch Money
   d. Hauschka-Boom

10. Jaguars running back Maurice Jones-Drew often used which shortened version his name as a nickname?

    a. Mojo
    b. Jonesy
    c. Reece
    d. J.D.

11. Which famous sportscaster memorably dubbed star Jacksonville wide receiver Andre "Bad Moon" Rison?

    a. ABC's Bob Costas
    b. Fox's John Madden
    c. NBC's Al Michaels
    d. ESPN's Chris Berman

12. After engaging in two memorable fights with his former Jaguars teammates as a newly traded member of the Los Angeles Rams, ex- Jaguars cornerback Jalen Ramsey earned the nickname "The Vengeful Ex"

    a. True
    b. False

13. Which food-based nickname was Jaguars defensive tackle Terrance Knighton more commonly known by?

    a. Bratwurst
    b. Hoagie
    c. Pot Roast
    d. Cheeseburger

14. Jaguars coach Jack Del Rio made numerous risky decisions during football games, which helped earn him which of the following nicknames?

    a. Black Jack
    b. Fearless
    c. Cajones
    d. The Gambler

15. Due to his risk-averse nature and unwillingness to throw long passes that the defense might be able to intercept, Jaguars quarterback Trent Edwards was given which derisive nickname?

    a. Hand Off
    b. The Regulator
    c. Captain Checkdown
    d. Wet Cement Trent

16. Jacksonville defensive end Calais Campbell was called "Uncle CC" by his young teammates because he was brought in to provide leadership and playoff experience while demonstrating how to act as a professional athlete.

    a. True
    b. False

17. In 2017, the members of the dominant Jacksonville secondary felt so good about how well they were playing that they put out a Twitter poll asking their followers to submit nickname suggestions for the group. Which of the following was NOT a suggestion they considered?

a. Steal Team 6

b. Kitty Claw Clampdown

c. The Jackson 5

d. Area 51

18. During the 2007 NFL season, the Jaguars' tendency to be involved in close games and complete numerous comeback victories resulted in which of the following nicknames for the squad?

a. The Crunch Time Brigade

b. The Last-Minute Wonders

c. The Jacksonville Cliffhangers

d. The Cardiac Jags

19. Jaguars tight end Marcedes Lewis was known by which of the following animal-based nicknames?

a. Panda Bear

b. The Giraffe

c. Big Dog

d. Foxcatcher

20. Jacksonville linebacker Paul Posluszny was jokingly referred to as "Buy A Vowel" by his teammates, because of the odd mix of consonants in his Polish last name.

a. True

b. False

QUIZ ANSWERS

1. D – The Jags

2. B – False

3. B – Family Ville

4. C – Wide receiver Torry Holt

5. A – He gave himself the nickname as a handle on the social media platform Twitter

6. A – Fragile Fred

7. B – False

8. D – Because Barwin mentioned Foles in response to an internet question about which football player had the largest genitalia

9. C – Hausch Money

10. A – Mojo

11. D – ESPN's Chris Berman

12. B – False

13. C – Pot Roast

14. A – Black Jack

15. C – Captain Checkdown

16. B – False

17. D – Area 51

18. D – The Cardiac Jags

19. C – Big Dog

20. B – False

DID YOU KNOW?

1. Jaguars quarterback Gardiner Minshew went so far as to file for a trademark on his nickname "Mississippi Mustache." Any apparel sold with that phrase on it would be subject to a lawsuit from Minshew.

2. The stern discipline and meticulousness of Jacksonville head coach Tom Coughlin led to players calling him not "Coach Coughlin" but "Colonel Coughlin," though not many would say it to his face.

3. Southern University uses the nickname "Jaguars," which means that when Jacksonville selected defensive end Chris White from the school in 1999, he became the first player in franchise history whose team nickname did not change upon joining the NFL.

4. When they formed one of Jacksonville's best ever wide receiver duos, Keenan McCardell and Jimmy Smith were often referred to as "Thunder and Lightning." McCardell's size led him to be "Thunder," while Smith's speed gave him the "Lightning" side of the equation.

5. Jacksonville running back Denard Robinson got his nickname, "Shoelace" at a young age. When Robinson started playing pee-wee football, he refused to tie his shoes, but excelled, nonetheless. He continued that practice in high school and college, and now wears shoes with a Velcro fastening in the NFL.

6. Leonard Fournette earned the nickname "Button" well before he arrived as a running back in Jacksonville. When he was a child, Fournette's grandmother thought his nose was small and "cute as a button," and the name just stuck after that.

7. The Jaguars defense, when playing well, is often referred to as "Sacksonville," a term used by announcers occasionally when a defender has taken down an opposing quarterback.

8. Jacksonville safety Andrew Wingard actually has several nicknames and at various times he may be addressed as "Dewey," "Sunshine," "Kid Rock," or "Tiny Thor." "Dewey" was given to him in childhood, but the rest reference Wingard's long blond hair.

9. Standing just 5-foot-7, Jaguars running back Maurice Jones-Drew was nonetheless a bruising, powerful runner. Because of this odd combination of traits, Jones-Drew was commonly dubbed "Pocket Hercules."

10. Jaguars running back Leonard Fournette gave quarterback Gardiner Minshew a new nickname in 2019 after witnessing Minshew stretching in the locker room while wearing his jock. Fournette dubbed the QB the "Jock Strap King," which quickly gained popularity with the media.

CHAPTER 4:

THE QUARTERBACKS

QUIZ TIME!

1. Which of these Jaguars quarterbacks has been sacked by opponents the most times during the span of their career (a total of 333 times sacked)?

   a. Mark Brunell
   b. David Garrard
   c. Byron Leftwich
   d. Blake Bortles

2. Blake Bortles holds the top-four spots on the Jaguars all-time list of most passing touchdowns thrown in a season?

   a. True
   b. False

3. Which quarterback has thrown the most intercepted passes in Jacksonville Jaguars franchise history?

   a. Blake Bortles
   b. Blaine Gabbert
   c. Chad Henne
   d. Mark Brunell

4. Who is the Jacksonville Jaguars' all-time career leader in most passing yards?

   a. Byron Leftwich
   b. Blake Bortles
   c. Mark Brunell
   d. Garner Minshew II

5. Which Jaguars player set the franchise record for most passing yards in a season by a Jacksonville quarterback; putting up 4,428?

   a. Blake Bortles
   b. David Garrard
   c. Gardner Minshew II
   d. Mark Brunell

6. How many players that have played quarterback for the Jaguars have been elected to the Pro Football Hall of Fame?

   a. The Jaguars have not had a quarterback who has been elected to the Hall of Fame
   b. One player - Mark Brunell
   c. Two players - Mark Brunell and Byron Leftwich
   d. Three players - Mark Brunell, Byron Leftwich, and Chad Henne

7. Inaugural team member Mark Brunell has played more games at QB for the Jaguars than any other player.

   a. True
   b. False

8. One journeyman Jacksonville quarterback has been a part of six NFL teams, more than any other among Jaguars quarterbacks. Who was this well-travelled player?

   a. David Garrard
   b. Cody Kessler
   c. Steve Beuerlein
   d. Byron Leftwich

9. Which two Jaguars were the youngest players in the team's history to start at quarterback at just 22 years old?

   a. Byron Leftwich and Gardner Minshew II
   b. David Garrard and Blaine Gabbert
   c. Blake Bortles and Cody Kessler
   d. Blake Bortles and Blaine Gabbert

10. Which Jacksonville quarterback was moved to the San Francisco 49ers to make way for new QB Blake Bortles after the Jaguars took Bortles in the first round of the NFL Draft in 2014?

    a. Byron Leftwich
    b. David Garrard
    c. Blaine Gabbert
    d. Chad Henne

11. How old was Jaguars legend Mark Brunell when he retired from his playing days in the NFL?

    a. 28 years old
    b. 36 years old
    c. 39 years old
    d. 41 years old

12. Jaguars QB Blaine Gabbert named previous QB Byron Leftwich as the godfather when his daughter Jessica was born in 2013.

    a. True
    b. False

13. The highest quarterback rating put up by a Jacksonville Jaguars for player who started a majority of games in the season was 80.9. Which QB scored this franchise high mark?

    a. Mark Brunell
    b. Blake Bortles
    c. David Garrard
    d. Gardner Minshew II

14. Which risk-averse Jaguars quarterback tossed only 10 interceptions while starting 16 games for the squad over the course of a regular season, easily setting the franchise record for fewest interceptions in a season?

    a. Mark Brunell
    b. Byron Leftwich
    c. Chad Henne
    d. David Garrard

15. Jaguars leader Mark Brunell holds the franchise's record for most rushing yards in a season by a quarterback, which he set in the team's inaugural 1995 season. How many yards did he rack up?

    a. 362 yards
    b. 480 yards

c. 703 yards

d. 855 yards

16. Jacksonville's Blaine Gabbert has won both a college national championship and a Super Bowl during his career.

   a. True

   b. False

17. Two players in NFL history have entered a game as a backup and tossed four touchdown passes with no interceptions. San Francisco 49ers Hall of Famer Steve Young is one; which Jacksonville quarterback is the other?

   a. Byron Leftwich

   b. David Garrard

   c. Gardner Minshew II

   d. Chad Henne

18. Which two Jacksonville quarterbacks have led the team to the most fourth quarter comeback victories in a single season, with each putting up four such wins?

   a. Mark Brunell and Byron Leftwich

   b. Blake Bortles and Gardner Minshew II

   c. Mark Brunell and Gardner Minshew II

   d. Byron Leftwich and David Garrard

19. How many times, combined, did prolific Jaguars quarterbacks Mark Brunell, Byron Leftwich and Gardner Minshew II throw for 25 (or more) touchdowns in a single season?

   a. Zero times

   b. Five times

c. Nine times

d. Twelve times

20. Among quarterbacks who have started at least five games with Jacksonville, Steve Beuerlein has the highest interception percentage, with 4.9% of his passes thrown being picked off.

   a. True

   b. False

QUIZ ANSWERS

1. A – Mark Brunell
2. B – False
3. D – Mark Brunell
4. C – Mark Brunell
5. A – Blake Bortles
6. A – The Jaguars have not had a quarterback who has been elected to the Hall of Fame
7. A – True
8. C – Steve Beuerlein
9. D – Blake Bortles and Blaine Gabbert
10. C – Blaine Gabbert
11. D – 41 years old
12. B – False
13. C – David Garrard
14. D – David Garrard
15. B – 480 yards
16. B – False
17. D – Chad Henne
18. A – Mark Brunell and Byron Leftwich
19. A – Zero times
20. A – True

DID YOU KNOW?

1. Blake Bortles owns the longest passing play in Jaguars history. He dropped back and found talented receiver Allen Robinson for a 90-yard touchdown toss in a 2015 matchup against the New Orleans Saints.

2. No Jaguars quarterback has ever been able to complete 70% of his passes in a season. The most accurate field general (who started at least half the team's games) was Gardner Minshew II. Minshew came the closest in 2020, when he hit 66.1%.

3. Mark Brunell could have used some better blocking when he lined up for the Jaguars in 2001. He was sacked a whopping 57 times when he dropped back to pass; the highest total in Jaguars history.

4. No retired Jaguars quarterbacks have played their entire NFL careers with Jacksonville. Current quarterbacks – Trevor Lawrence, Gardner Minshew II and Jake Luton – have not played anywhere else in their NFL careers, but it remains to be seen if they will retire as Jaguars.

5. Quarterback continuity reigned in Jacksonville for nearly the first decade of the franchise's history. Mark Brunell spent nine years with the franchise from 1995-2003 before giving way to Byron Leftwich and David Garrard, who took the franchise through the next seven years.

6. In 2014, Jaguars rookie quarterback Blake Bortles led the largest comeback win in Jacksonville history. Down 21-0 against the New York Giants, Bortles refused to give up and spurred the team to a 25-24 triumph.

7. There was much excitement in Jacksonville when former Super Bowl MVP Nick Foles signed an $88 million contract to come to Jacksonville in 2019, and it continued when Foles led a touchdown drive in the first quarter of his first game against the Kansas City Chiefs. However, soon after that he fractured his clavicle, missed most of the season, and was dealt to the Chicago Bears the following offseason.

8. Former Jacksonville quarterback Blaine Gabbert is an avid fisherman and spends a good deal of his time in the offseason fly fishing, deep sea fishing and documenting his catches on Instagram.

9. In 2019 and 2020, a phenomenon called "Minshew Mania" hit Jacksonville and the rest of the NFL. This was all because of quirky Jaguars QB Gardner Minshew II, whose combination of talent (a team record 88% completion percentage in his first game), and style (a propensity for wearing cutoff jean shorts and a headband, along with a mustache that has its own Twitter account) took the city by storm.

10. Jaguars quarterback David Garrard used his connections with the team to help him with a very special event: his marriage proposal. Garrard popped the question to his girlfriend Mary Knox prior to a preseason game in 2002,

and the moment was shown to everyone in attendance on the Jumbotron at the stadium.

CHAPTER 5:

THE PASS CATCHERS

QUIZ TIME!

1. Three pass catchers have recorded 30 or more career touchdown catches for the Jaguars. Which one of them has the most?

    a. Wide receiver Keenan McCardell

    b. Tight end Marcedes Lewis

    c. Wide receiver Jimmy Smith

    d. Keenan McCardell and Jimmy Smith are tied for the lead

2. No one in Jaguars history is within 350 receptions of wide receiver Jimmy Smith at the top of Jacksonville's record book.

    a. True

    b. False

3. Who is the Jaguars single season leader in receiving touchdowns scored with 14?

    a. Wide receiver Reggie Williams in the 2007 season

    b. Wide receiver Allen Robinson in the 2015 season

c. Tight end Marcedes Lewis in the 2010 season

d. Wide receiver Jimmy Smith in the 2001 season

4. Who holds the all-time career franchise record for receiving yardage for the Jaguars and is the only man to notch beyond 10,000 receiving yards with the franchise?

a. Running back Maurice Jones-Drew

b. Tight end Marcedes Lewis

c. Wide receiver Jimmy Smith

d. Wide receiver Allen Hurns

5. Which of the following is NOT a true fact about Jacksonville Jaguars wide receiver Andre Rison?

a. His girlfriend, famous rapper Lisa Lopes, once set fire to Rison's house

b. He has won both a Super Bowl in the NFL and a Grey Cup in the CFL

c. He set an NFL record by recording a touchdown with seven different teams

d. He once celebrated a touchdown by chugging a beer on the sidelines, instead of Gatorade

6. No Jaguars with at least 100 receptions have averaged 15 yards per catch over their careers. Which wide receiver has shown the best big play ability, hitting an average of 14.3 yards per catch?

a. Allen Robinson

b. Cecil Shorts

c. D.J. Chark

d. Jimmy Smith

7. Jaguars head coach Doug Marrone hired former Jacksonville pass catcher Keenan McCardell to be his wide receivers coach from 2017-2020.

   a. True
   b. False

8. Which Jaguars pass catcher has played more NFL games with the franchise than any other player, totaling 171 over the years?

   a. Wide receiver Keenan McCardell
   b. Wide receiver Jimmy Smith
   c. Tight end Marcedes Lewis
   d. Tight end Rich Griffith

9. Three non-wide receivers have over 275 career receptions for the Jacksonville Jaguars. Which of the following players is NOT among that club?

   a. Running back Fred Taylor
   b. Tight end Marcedes Lewis
   c. Running back Maurice Jones-Drew
   d. Tight end Kyle Brady

10. Despite all his accomplishments, Jimmy Smith has more career fumbles than any other Jaguars wide receiver. How many times did he cough up the ball?

    a. 12 times
    b. 16 times
    c. 22 times
    d. 27 times

11. According to Spotrac.com which current Jaguars wide receiver is playing for the team on the contract with the highest total value at $14.25 million?

   a. Marvin Jones Jr.
   b. DJ Chark Jr.
   c. Jamal Agnew
   d. Laviska Shenault Jr.

12. No current wide receiver in the NFL is taller than Jacksonville's Collin Johnson, who is 6'6".

   a. True
   b. False

13. How many Jaguars tight ends have caught over 200 passes for the club during their careers?

   a. One tight end: Marcedes Lewis
   b. Two tight ends: Marcedes Lewis and Kyle Brady
   c. Three tight ends: Marcedes Lewis, Kyle Brady, and Pete Mitchell
   d. Five tight ends: Marcedes Lewis, Kyle Brady, Pete Mitchell, Julius Thomas, and George Wrightster

14. Which two teammates posted the highest combined receiving yardage total in a season for the Jaguars, totaling 2,527 yards together?

   a. Allen Robinson and Allen Hurns in the 2015 season
   b. Cecil Shorts and Justin Blackmon in the 2012 season
   c. Jimmy Smith and Keenan McCardell in the 1997 season

d. Jimmy Smith and Keenan McCardell in the 1999 season

15. Which of the following is NOT an NFL record held by Jaguars wide receiver Torry Holt?

    a. Most yards per play gained in a single game, with 63 on September 24, 2000
    b. Most catches in a decade, with 868 between 2000-09
    c. Most receiving yards per game for a career, with 79.8
    d. Most receiving yards in a decade, with 12,594 between 2000-09

16. Speedy Jacksonville Jaguars wide receiver Dede Westbrook once participated in an unusual race in which he competed in a 40-yard dash against a racehorse and a motorcycle. Westbrook defeated the horse but finished behind the motorcycle.

    a. True
    b. False

17. Which Jaguar recorded the most catches in one season for the team, when he hauled in 116 passes for the squad?

    a. Jimmy Smith
    b. Allen Robinson
    c. Keenan McCardell
    d. D.J. Chark

18. The talented Jimmy Smith had sushi restaurants in Jacksonville naming a special roll in his honor. Which ingredients could be found in "The Jimmy Smith Roll" at Ichiban Japanese Steakhouse in Jacksonville?

a. Shrimp tempura, cucumber, and caviar, with soy sauce

b. Eel, asparagus, avocado, and mango, with wasabi

c. Smoked salmon, cream cheese, crabstick, and scallions, with spicy mayo sauce

d. Soft shell crab, tuna, tomato, and yam, with horseradish

19. Which two teammates posted the highest touchdown reception total in a season for the Jaguars, converting 24 passes into scores?

    a. Wide receivers Jimmy Smith and Keenan McCardell in the 2001 season

    b. Wide receivers Allen Robinson and Allen Hurns in the 2015 season

    c. Tight end Marcedes Lewis and wide receiver Mike Sims-Walker in the 2009 season

    d. Wide receivers D.J. Chark and Dede Westbrook in the 2019 season

20. Tight end Marcedes Lewis played for 12 seasons with Jacksonville and did not catch his first playoff touchdown pass until his final game with the team.

    a. True

    b. False

QUIZ ANSWERS

1. C – Wide receiver Jimmy Smith

2. A – True

3. B – Wide receiver Allen Robinson in the 2015 season

4. C – Wide receiver Jimmy Smith

5. D – He once celebrated a touchdown by chugging a beer on the sidelines instead of Gatorade

6. D – Jimmy Smith

7. A – True

8. B – Wide receiver Jimmy Smith

9. D – Tight end Kyle Brady

10. A – 12 times

11. C – Jamal Agnew

12. A – True

13. B – Two tight ends: Marcedes Lewis and Kyle Brady

14. D – Jimmy Smith and Keenan McCardell in the 1999 season

15. C – Most receiving yards per game for a career with 79.8

16. B – False

17. A – Jimmy Smith

18. C – Smoked salmon, cream cheese, crabstick and scallions with spicy mayo sauce

19. B – Wide receivers Allen Robinson and Allen Hurns in the 2015 season

20. A – True

DID YOU KNOW?

1. Jaguars icon Jimmy Smith ranks 24th on the all-time list for most receiving yards in the history of the NFL, with 12,287. Smith is sandwiched between Brandon Marshall and Charlie Joiner on the list.

2. The single-game record for most receptions in Jacksonville Jaguars history was actually set in just their second season of existence. Keenan McCardell reeled in 16 passes against the St. Louis Rams in 1996 to set the mark.

3. Before his years in Jacksonville, wide receiver Keenan McCardell won a Super Bowl ring with the Washington Redskins despite never playing a game for them. After spending his entire rookie season on the IR, McCardell was honored as a champion and then cut by the team.

4. Only 19 tight ends in NFL history have recorded more than 500 pass receptions. The Jaguars boast none of those tight ends. Marcedes Lewis, who had 375 catches with Jacksonville and 403 overall, came the closest to that elite level.

5. Jaguars wide receiver Marqise Lee is fluent in sign language. Lee learned this skill as a child because both his mother and father were deaf and needed to teach their children to communicate with them.

6. Jacksonville tight end Marcedes Lewis is tied for the team record for most receiving touchdowns in a single game

with three. This is just two off of the NFL's overall record of five. Lewis went off against the Baltimore Ravens in 2017, hauling in scoring passes of 4, 17, and 30 yards from Jaguars quarterback Blake Bortles that day.

7. Allen Hurns was the first Jaguars receiver to earn a starting spot for a season opening game in his rookie year. Hurns did not disappoint as he scored touchdowns on both of the first two passes thrown to him by quarterback Chad Henne that day.

8. In 2007, Jaguars wide receiver Matt Jones made a public vow not to shave his beard until he scored a touchdown. The beard grew until week 8 when Jones caught a touchdown pass against the Tampa Bay Buccaneers.

9. Former Jacksonville tight end Kyle Brady owns a few impressive licenses beyond a simple driver's license. Brady also has a pilot's license, a financial advisor license, and a license to practice law.

10. In the 2001 season, Jacksonville wide receiver Jimmy Smith caught at least five passes in every single game, setting an NFL record which has since been tied by Antonio Brown and Pierre Garcon.

CHAPTER 6:

RUNNING WILD

QUIZ TIME!

1. Who holds the Jaguars' single-season franchise rushing yardage record after racking up 1,606 yards on the ground?

    a. Maurice Jones-Drew

    b. Leonard Fournette

    c. Fred Taylor

    d. James Stewart

2. It is a Jaguars tradition for every running back to tap his helmet against the helmets of the starting offensive linemen following the warmup before a game.

    a. True

    b. False

3. Which running back has accumulated the most carries for Jacksonville without ever scoring a rushing touchdown with 98 rushes?

    a. Vaughn Dunbar

    b. Toby Gerhart

c. Deji Karim

d. Elvis Joseph

4. Jacksonville RB Maurice Jones-Drew finished second in the NFL Offensive Rookie of the Year voting in 2006, behind which winning player?

a. Running back Reggie Bush of the New Orleans Saints

b. Quarterback Vince Young of the Tennessee Titans

c. Quarterback Jay Cutler of the Denver Broncos

d. Wide receiver Marques Colston of the New Orleans Saints

5. How many running backs have carried the ball over 1,000 times for the Jaguars?

a. One running back: Fred Taylor

b. Two running backs: Fred Taylor and Maurice Jones-Drew

c. Three running backs: Fred Taylor, Maurice Jones-Drew, and Leonard Fournette

d. Five running backs: Fred Taylor, Maurice Jones-Drew, Leonard Fournette, T.J. Yeldon, and James Stewart

6. No Jaguars running back with at least 16 games played has averaged over 100 yards per game during his career. Fred Taylor is the closest; what is his average?

a. 80.5 yards per game

b. 88.4 yards per game

c. 92.6 yards per game

d. 98.1 yards per game

7. Maurice Jones-Drew has 68 rushing touchdowns with the Jaguars, which is more than the next three highest Jacksonville running backs combined.

    a. True
    b. False

8. In which season did Maurice Jones-Drew record an astonishing 5.7 yards per carry for Jacksonville?

    a. 2006
    b. 2008
    c. 2011
    d. 2013

9. Which Jacksonville running back (with at least 300 carries) has the highest career yards gained per attempt with 4.6?

    a. Natrone Means
    b. Maurice Jones-Drew
    c. Leonard Fournette
    d. Fred Taylor

10. Current Jaguars RB James Robinson recorded his first NFL touchdown against which NFL team?

    a. Houston Texans
    b. Indianapolis Colts
    c. Tennessee Titans
    d. Kansas City Chiefs

11. How many of the Jaguars' top-10 seasons for rushing touchdowns were recorded by the great Maurice Jones-Drew?

a. Two seasons

b. Four seasons

c. Five seasons

d. Seven seasons

12. Former Jaguars running back James Stewart decided to become a personal trainer in retirement and opened up a studio in Jacksonville called "Studio 33," which is a nod to his uniform number as a player.

a. True

b. False

13. Which Jacksonville running back has the most career fumbles with 26 dropped balls?

a. Denard Robinson

b. Natrone Means

c. Fred Taylor

d. Chris Ivory

14. Which Jaguar had the highest single season rushing yards per game, averaging 107.6 per contest?

a. Maurice Jones-Drew in the 2011 season

b. Leonard Fournette in the 2017 season

c. James Stewart in the 1998 season

d. Fred Taylor in the 2000 season

15. Which of the following is NOT a true fact about longtime Jaguars running back Greg Jones?

a. He is cousins with former heavyweight boxing champion of the world Joe Frazier

b. He was at one point the highest paid fullback in NFL history

c. He injured his ACL twice, once in college and once while with the Jaguars

d. He now owns an autobody repair shop called Jones Dents & Dings

16. Jaguars rookie running back Leonard Fournette had an up and down season in his first year with the club. Fournette started strong, scoring a touchdown in each of his first six games, but then missed three weeks in a row with an injury, a bye and an inactive designation for breaking a club rule.

a. True

b. False

17. During his magical 2011 season, Maurice Jones-Drew was the focal point of the Jacksonville offense. What percentage of the team's offensive yards did he account for that year?

a. 38.5% of their yards

b. 42.6% of their yards

c. 47.7% of their yards

d. 52.3% of their yards

18. Which two Jacksonville running backs caught some backlash from Tom Coughlin for looking too disinterested while on the bench during a game, with Coughlin saying that their behavior was "disrespectful, selfish … unbecoming that of a professional football player"?

a. Leonard Fournette and T.J. Yeldon
b. Fred Taylor and Maurice Jones-Drew
c. Natrone Means and James Stewart
d. Chris Ivory and Carlos Hyde

19. In the 2020 season, Jaguars RB James Robinson became just the fourth undrafted rookie in NFL history to generate a 1,000-yard rushing season in his debut year. Which of the following players did Robinson NOT join in that accomplishment?

a. Phillip Lindsay of the Denver Broncos
b. LeGarrette Blount of the Tampa Bay Buccaneers
c. Dominic Rhodes of the Indianapolis Colts
d. Arian Foster of the Houston Texans

20. No Jaguars running back has ever been named as a first team All-Pro member.

a. True
b. False

QUIZ ANSWERS

1. A – Maurice Jones-Drew

2. B – False

3. C – Deji Karim

4. B – Quarterback Vince Young of the Tennessee Titans

5. B – Two running backs: Fred Taylor and Maurice Jones-Drew

6. A – 80.5 yards per game

7. B – False

8. A – 2006

9. D – Fred Taylor

10. C – Tennessee Titans

11. B – Four seasons

12. A – True

13. C – Fred Taylor

14. D – Fred Taylor in the 2000 season

15. D – He now owns an autobody repair shop called Jones Dents & Dings

16. A – True

17. C – 47.7% of their yards

18. A – Leonard Fournette and T.J. Yeldon

19. D – Arian Foster of the Houston Texans

20. B – False

DID YOU KNOW?

1. No running backs who have played for the Jaguars have been enshrined in the Pro Football Hall of Fame.

2. In 2001, Fred Taylor's reputation was hurt among Jacksonville fans who questioned his toughness. This was in large part because Jaguars head coach Tom Coughlin posted Taylor as "questionable" on the injury report from week four through the end of the season, even though Coughlin knew in week three that Taylor was done for the year.

3. Eleven times in NFL history, a running back has scored 20 or more rushing touchdowns in a single season. Maurice Jones-Drew got the closest for Jacksonville when he tallied 15 rushing scores in 2009.

4. Jaguars running back Denard Robinson was actually a quarterback at the University of Michigan. Robinson set all sorts of NCAA records during his career, including the most career rushing yards ever racked up by a quarterback, and the only season in which a player ever recorded both 2,500 yards passing and 1,500 yards rushing.

5. Jacksonville running back Leonard Fournette holds the NFL record as the youngest player to score a rushing touchdown that was at least 90 yards long. Fournette was just 22 years old when he accomplished this feat.

6. In 2013, the year he finished his time with the Jacksonville Jaguars, running back Maurice Jones-Drew went back to UCLA to finish his bachelor's degree. Despite his wife, children, and multi-millionaire status, Jones-Drew chose to live on campus in a dormitory with other students.

7. On October 12, 1997, Jaguars running back James Stewart set two team records in an epic performance against the Philadelphia Eagles. Stewart rushed for five touchdowns in the game, accounting for 30 points, both of which still stand as franchise highs.

8. Jacksonville running back Rashad Jennings not only appeared on the television show Dancing with the Stars, but won his season alongside professional dancer Emma Slater. Jennings joined fellow NFL stars Emmitt Smith, Donald Driver and Hines Ward as winners of the show.

9. Former Jaguars running back James Stewart had his career cut short as part of a bounty program run by notorious coach Gregg Williams. Buffalo Bills safety Coy Wire admitted "I shattered James Stewart's shoulder and he never played again. I was showered with praise for that. It's a shame that's how it was. Now I see how wrong that was."

10. In retirement, Jaguars icon Maurice Jones-Drew became a television analyst, but not for the Jacksonville or Oakland, the two teams he had played with. Rather, Jones-Drew returned to Los Angeles, where he had attended college, to work for the L.A. Rams.

CHAPTER 7:

IN THE TRENCHES

QUIZ TIME!

1. One Jaguars defender holds the team record by notching four sacks in a single game. Which defensive player was it?

    a. Defensive end Yannick Ngakoue
    b. Linebacker Kevin Hardy
    c. Defensive end Calais Campbell
    d. Defensive tackle John Henderson

2. The 2016 Jacksonville Jaguars hold the NFL record for the heaviest combined weight of all starting offensive and defensive linemen.

    a. True
    b. False

3. Who is the Jaguars' all-time franchise leader in sacks, having taken down opposing quarterbacks 55 times?

    a. Defensive tackle Gary Walker
    b. Linebacker Daryl Smith

c. Defensive end Tony Brackens

d. Defensive end Yannick Ngakoue

4. The Jaguars have always put a premium on offensive line talent, but which of the following players did the Jaguars NOT invest a first-round draft pick on to add the stout blocker to their team?

   a. Tony Boselli

   b. Eugene Monroe

   c. Luke Joeckel

   d. Maurice Williams

5. Which offensive lineman has played more games on the offensive side of the Jaguars' line of scrimmage than anyone else?

   a. Center Brad Meester

   b. Guard Vince Manuwai

   c. Tackle Tony Boselli

   d. Guard Tyler Shatley

6. Which defensive lineman has played more games on the defensive side of the Jaguars' line of scrimmage than anyone else?

   a. Tackle John Henderson

   b. End Paul Spicer

   c. Tackle Tyson Alualu

   d. End Rob Meier

7. Jacksonville offensive tackle Eugene Monroe was the youngest sibling in a family that included 15 other children; 10 brothers and 5 sisters.

a. True

b. False

8. Which Jaguars defender showed the best nose for the ball, by leading the team in most career forced fumbles with 27?

   a. Linebacker Kevin Hardy

   b. Defensive end Tony Brackens

   c. Cornerback Rashean Mathis

   d. Defensive end Joel Smeenge

9. Quarterback Mark Brunell tops the record books for most fumbles recovered for the Jaguars, but he tended to be cleaning up his own mess. Which defender has created the most turnovers for Jacksonville by scooping up an opponent's fumble?

   a. Strong safety Travis Davis

   b. Strong safety Donovan Darius

   c. Defensive end Tony Brackens

   d. Linebacker Telvin Smith

10. Why did star Jaguars defensive tackle Tony Brackens, who played his entire career with the club, claim that he was retiring from football?

   a. Because the Jaguars could not afford to keep him under the salary cap and Brackens did not want to play for another team

   b. Because he experienced persistent symptoms after suffering a concussion during a game in 2004

c. Because he did not approve of some rule changes made by the NFL that Brackens felt made the game less enjoyable

d. Because he had been offered the opportunity to become the head coach at his alma mater, the University of Texas, and did not want to risk losing that chance

11. Jaguars mainstay John Henderson played over 120 NFL games as a defensive tackle with the club. Where does he rank in games played all time for Jacksonville?

a. 2nd overall
b. Tied for 5th overall
c. 10th overall
d. Tied for 13th overall

12. After his playing career ended, Jaguars guard Uche Nwaneri started his own YouTube channel called "The Observant Lineman" to discuss sports, games, and comics.

a. True
b. False

13. Which two current Jaguars defensive linemen have the longest tenure in Jacksonville at four years apiece?

a. End Josh Allen and tackle DaVon Hamilton
b. Tackles Daniel Ross and Doug Costin
c. Ends Jihad Ward and Adam Gotsis
d. Ends Lerentee McCray and Dawuane Smoot

14. Which of the following is NOT a real business opened by Jaguars defensive lineman John Henderson in his retirement?

a. A clothing store for large men called "4 Big Men by Big Hen"

b. A fitness center called "Hendo's Get Swole"

c. A night club called "Aleviar's VIP Lounge and Jazz Bar"

d. A restaurant called "Big John's Crumpy's Wings & Things"

15. Which of All Pro offensive tackle Tony Boselli's body parts sustained multiple injuries on the playing field, eventually forcing him into retirement?

a. His knee

b. His back

c. His ankle

d. His shoulder

16. Defensive end Calais Campbell not only played excellent football for Jacksonville, but also toured as a standup comedian in the offseason during his time with the Jaguars.

a. True

b. False

17. Which of the following is NOT a hobby that longtime Jaguars center Brad Meester likes to pursue in his retirement?

a. Riding motorcycles

b. Hunting alligators

c. Restoring tractors

d. Collecting sports cards

18. Offensive tackle Tony Boselli accomplished a lot of "firsts" for the Jaguars. Which of the following is NOT a real "first" that Boselli achieved?

    a. First Jaguar to earn a Pro Bowl berth every year of his career
    b. First Jaguar to have a burger named after him at McDonald's restaurant
    c. First player chosen by the Houston Texans in their 2002 expansion draft
    d. First player elected to be in the Pride of the Jaguars

19. While playing for the Jaguars, guard Ben Coleman invested some of his salary into several locations of which popular ice cream franchise?

    a. Ben & Jerry's
    b. Dairy Queen
    c. Cold Stone Creamery
    d. Baskin-Robbins

20. Jaguars defensive tackle Marcus Stroud is a self-described "adrenaline junkie" who requested (and received) a clause in his contract allowing him to participate in activities such as bungee jumping, skydiving, and motorcycle racing. Stroud was forced to stipulate that the Jaguars would not be liable to pay him if he suffered an injury during any of those activities.

    a. True
    b. False

QUIZ ANSWERS

1. C – Defensive end Calais Campbell

2. B – False

3. C – Defensive end Tony Brackens

4. D – Maurice Williams

5. A – Center Brad Meester

6. D – End Rob Meier

7. A – True

8. B – Defensive end Tony Brackens

9. C – Defensive end Tony Brackens

10. C – Because he did not approve of some rule changes made by the NFL that Brackens felt made the game less enjoyable

11. C – 10th overall

12. A – True

13. D – Ends Lerentee McCray and Dawuane Smoot

14. B – A fitness center called "Hendo's Get Swole"

15. D – His shoulder

16. B – False

17. D – Collecting sports cards

18. A – First Jaguar to earn a Pro Bowl berth every year of his career

19. C – Cold Stone Creamery

20. B – False

DID YOU KNOW?

1. Eight players share the Jacksonville record for most safeties created, as no athlete has recorded more than one. All eight of these players are either linebackers or defensive linemen.

2. Jacksonville left tackle Tony Boselli and the quarterback he protected, Mark Brunell, continued their close relationship even after their playing days were done. The two former teammates have been partners in Mattress Firm bedding company, Whataburger restaurant, and on a football coaching staff at a local school.

3. Jaguars defensive end Paul Spicer earned a role as a security guard in a movie called "The Year of Getting to Know Us." The movie starred Tom Arnold and Jimmy Fallon, and featured Spicer throwing Fallon off of an airplane in a scene at Jacksonville International Airport.

4. When Brandon Linder signed a new contract with Jacksonville in 2017, he set the NFL record for the biggest contract ever inked by a center. Linder's deal was for five years, and it was worth $51.7 million.

5. Former Jaguars offensive tackle Eugene Monroe is a very high-profile advocate of the use of cannabis. Even while still playing in the league, Monroe campaigned for the NFL to allow its use for pain management, arguing it was a healthier alternative to common use of opioids. Since

retiring, Monroe has continued to speak about, write about and donate money to this cause.

6. In the midst of a heated dispute with the team, defensive end Yannick Ngakoue once told the son of owner Shahid Khan "Just trade me" on Twitter after Jacksonville had used the franchise tag on Ngakoue instead. Ngakoue was eventually shipped to the Minnesota Vikings for draft picks.

7. Jaguars offensive tackle Leon Searcy has appeared in two different documentaries within the popular ESPN 30 for 30 series. Searcy contributed interviews for "The U" about The University of Miami Hurricanes, his alma mater, and "Broke" about the financial problems of former athletes.

8. One of the most productive duos in Jacksonville history was the defensive tackle combination of John Henderson and Marcus Stroud. Thanks to their Florida-based location and ability to wreak havoc, the pair was known together as "Hurricane Henderstroud."

9. Defensive tackle Rob Meier was a star for Jacksonville for almost a full decade in the 2000's despite being chosen in the seventh round of the NFL Draft. Meier, who was born in Vancouver, British Columbia, was also the first overall pick in the CFL Draft but despite being selected by his hometown BC Lions, he never suited up in that league.

10. When center Brad Meester joined the Jaguars in 2000, he started for them immediately … and didn't stop for a long time. Meester set the franchise record by starting his first

92 games in a row; a streak that was only broken by an injury suffered six seasons later.

CHAPTER 8:

THE BACK SEVEN

QUIZ TIME!

11. Which Jaguars cornerback is the franchise's all-time leader in interceptions with 30; double the number of the next closest Jag?

    a. Jalen Ramsey
    b. A.J. Bouye
    c. Rashean Mathis
    d. Aaron Beasley

12. During the 2010's poker craze, members of Jacksonville's secondary and linebacking corps held a weekly game where, rather than playing for money, the losers had to tweet embarrassing things about themselves or flattering things about the winners.

    a. True
    b. False

13. Two Jaguars players share the team's lead for most interceptions returned for a touchdown, with three apiece. Who are they?

a. Cornerback Aaron Beasley and defensive end Tony Brackens

b. Linebacker Paul Posluszny and defensive back Barry Church

c. Cornerback Jalen Ramsey and linebacker Myles Jack

d. Cornerback Rashean Mathis and linebacker Telvin Smith

14. Sacks are usually not a high priority for defensive backs in most coaching systems, which is primarily why no Jaguars DB has more than the 7.5 sacks put up by which of the following?

a. Cornerback Aaron Beasley

b. Safety Donovin Darius

c. Cornerback Jalen Ramsey

d. Safety Johnathan Cyprien

15. The initials in popular Jaguars cornerback A.J. Bouye's name actually stand for what?

a. Anthony Jr.

b. Adam Joseph

c. Arlandus Jacob

d. A'Shawn Jerome

16. The Jaguars' record for most tackles made in a single season is 231. Which player set that high mark for the franchise?

a. Linebacker Myles Jack

b. Safety Tashaun Gibson

c. Cornerback Jalen Ramsey

d. Linebacker Paul Posluszny

17. Jacksonville safety Johnathan Cyprien loves snorkeling and is working towards becoming certified in scuba so that he can explore further underwater.

a. True

b. False

18. Who was the first player for Jacksonville to make at least 100 tackles for four straight seasons with the franchise?

a. Linebacker Akin Ayodele

b. Safety Donovin Darius

c. Linebacker Kevin Hardy

d. Linebacker Paul Posluszny

19. Jaguars cornerback Rashean Mathis set the NCAA Division I records for most interceptions in a single season and most interceptions in a career while playing at Bethune-Cookman University. How many of each did he record?

a. 9 in a season and 29 in his career

b. 11 in a season and 38 in his career

c. 14 in a season and 31 in his career

d. 17 in a season and 43 in his career

20. Which Jaguars linebacker was the first player on the defensive side of the ball to become an opening day starter as a rookie for the club?

a. Paul Posluszny

b. Myles Jack

c. Telvin Smith

d. Kevin Hardy

21. Jaguars mainstay Rashean Mathis played over 135 NFL games as a cornerback with the club. Where does he rank in games played all time for Jacksonville?

a. 3rd overall

b. 7th overall

c. Tied for 10th overall

d. Tied for 15th overall

22. Years after his playing and coaching careers were both over, Jacksonville safety Gerald Sensabaugh became a became a competitive fisherman and then ran for mayor of Sullivan County, Tennessee.

a. True

b. False

23. Which of the following positions has popular Jaguars linebacker Bryce Paup NOT held within the coaching world after retiring from his playing career?

a. Assistant linebackers coach for the Jacksonville Jaguars

b. Linebackers coach at De Pere High School

c. Defensive line coach at the University of Northern Iowa

d. Head coach at Green Bay Southwest High School

24. Which of these current Jaguars defensive backs has been with the team for five seasons; the longest current tenure in Jacksonville's secondary?

a. Andrew Wingard
b. Tre Herndon
c. Jarrod Wilson
d. Sidney Jones

25. Which Jacksonville linebacker and head coach once had a major dispute during a team meeting that led to the linebacker being sent home for a couple of days and then demoted to a backup role on the field?

a. Linebacker Myles Jack and head coach Doug Marrone
b. Linebacker Telvin Smith and head coach Gus Bradley
c. Linebacker Paul Posluszny and head coach Tom Coughlin
d. Linebacker Mike Peterson and head coach Jack Del Rio

26. In 1996, cornerback Mickey Washington established the "Jags Time" tradition, wherein he donated his gold pocket watch upon retirement to the next cornerback to take up the mantle for Jacksonville. To this day, the watch hangs in a cornerback's locker and he must pass it on if he retires, is traded, cut, or signs elsewhere.

a. True
b. False

27. Against which opposing team did Jacksonville cornerback Rashean Mathis notch two interceptions (including one that he ran back for a touchdown) during a 2008 playoff game?

a. Pittsburgh Steelers

b. New England Patriots

c. Indianapolis Colts

d. Denver Broncos

28. Linebacker Telvin Smith played his entire NFL career with the Jacksonville Jaguars after they selected him in the fifth round in 2014 out of Florida State University. How long did that career last?

a. 3 seasons

b. 5 seasons

c. 8 seasons

d. 11 seasons

29. Longtime Jaguars linebacker Daryl Smith eventually left the club as a free agent in order to replace which recently retired legendary linebacker?

a. Brian Urlacher on the Chicago Bears

b. Junior Seau on the New England Patriots

c. Ray Lewis on the Baltimore Ravens

d. Zach Thomas on the Miami Dolphins

30. Jacksonville linebacker Mike Peterson is the older brother of *an* NFL running back named Adrian Peterson, but not *the* superstar Adrian Peterson most known for his time with the Minnesota Vikings.

a. True

b. False

QUIZ ANSWERS

1. C – Rashean Mathis

2. B – False

3. D – Cornerback Rashean Mathis and linebacker Telvin Smith

4. A – Cornerback Aaron Beasley

5. C – Arlandus Jacob

6. D – Linebacker Paul Posluszny

7. A – True

8. A – Linebacker Akin Ayodele

9. C – 14 in a season and 31 in his career

10. D – Kevin Hardy

11. B – 7th overall

12. A – True

13. A – Assistant linebackers coach for the Jacksonville Jaguars

14. C – Jarrod Wilson

15. D – Linebacker Mike Peterson and head coach Jack Del Rio

16. B – False

17. A – Pittsburgh Steelers

18. B – 5 seasons

19. C – Ray Lewis on the Baltimore Ravens

20. A – True

DID YOU KNOW?

1. Passes defended is a stat that the NFL began using at the turn of the century. With 104 recorded, cornerback Rashean Mathis has dominated the statistic for the Jaguars, having more than twice as many as his closest competition (cornerback Fernando Bryant).

2. In 2016, Jaguars safety Johnathan Cyprien was a force on the field with 128 tackles made. Pro Football Focus graded him at 98.8 as a run-stopper; a mark that no safety before or since has achieved.

3. Linebacker Daryl Smith is the all-time leading tackler for the Jaguars franchise. Smith played in Jacksonville for nine seasons and racked up 1,089 tackles during that time.

4. Cornerback Jalen Ramsey was never shy with his opinion while playing for the Jaguars. In a 2018 interview, Ramsey said of quarterback Josh Allen, who had been drafted by the Buffalo Bills, "I think Allen is trash. I don't care what nobody say. He's trash … that's a stupid draft pick to me."

5. Expectations were high for linebacker/defensive end Dante Fowler after the Jaguars drafted him third overall in 2015. However, those expectations were dashed on the very first day of minicamp when Fowler suffered a torn ACL that forced him to miss his entire rookie year.

6. Jaguars cornerback Jason Craft was smart enough to decipher legendary quarterback Peyton Manning's audible calls during a game against the Indianapolis Colts in 2012. Unfortunately, he was also arrogant enough to brag about his discovery, which Manning took advantage of to mislead Jacksonville's defense and give the Colts an easy touchdown.

7. No defensive backs who have played for the Jaguars have been enshrined in the Pro Football Hall of Fame. No linebackers have made the cut either.

8. Jacksonville linebacker Russell Allen had a scary moment when he suffered a stroke on the field during a December 15, 2013 game against the Buffalo Bills. Though Allen would recover, he would never play football again as doctors warned him that it would no longer be safe to collide with other players.

9. In his retirement, Jaguars linebacker Kevin Hardy remained in Jacksonville and started a business called Dream Nightclub in South Beach. He chose the name because he felt that "reality is overrated."

10. Safety Donovin Darius spent most of his career in Jacksonville, and also decided to go back to school there. Darius attended Jacksonville University to add an MBA to his resume, and now serves on the NFL Players Association Executive Committee.

CHAPTER 9:

WHERE'D THEY COME FROM?

QUIZ TIME!

1. Where was legendary Jaguars wide receiver Jimmy Smith born?

    a. Detroit, Michigan

    b. Orlando, Florida

    c. Brooklyn, New York

    d. Oakland, California

2. Jaguars cornerback Rashean Mathis, who played for a decade with the team, went to high school in Jacksonville, Florida.

    a. True

    b. False

3. In their first ever NFL Draft, the Jaguars selected 10 players. Colleges from which state provided most of their inaugural draft class?

    a. New York

    b. Florida

c. South Carolina

d. California

4. Which of the following players has NOT been involved in a trade between the Jaguars and their fellow Florida footballers, the Miami Dolphins?

a. Center Brad Meester

b. Tight end Julius Thomas

c. Left tackle Branden Albert

d. Guard Justin Smiley

5. From which team did the Jaguars acquire useful defensive tackle Marcell Dareus in a 2017 swap?

a. Green Bay Packers

b. Buffalo Bills

c. New England Patriots

d. Los Angeles Rams

6. Which of the following is NOT an actual college program that Jacksonville drafted a player from during their first five NFL Drafts?

a. Missouri Western State Griffons

b. Middle Tennessee State Blue Raiders

c. Delaware Tech Devils

d. Augustana Vikings

7. The Jaguars have drafted more players from the Michigan State Spartans than from the Michigan Wolverines over the course of their history.

a. True

b. False

8. Which high profile player dealt in a trade from the Jaguars to the San Francisco 49ers franchise later went on to win a Super Bowl with the Tampa Bay Buccaneers?

    a. Quarterback Blaine Gabbert
    b. Running back Leonard Fournette
    c. Defensive end Calais Campbell
    d. Cornerback Jalen Ramsey

9. One of the Jaguars' best trades saw them acquire just a fourth-round draft pick. This was notable because they were able to ship quarterback Nick Foles, and the remainder of his massive $88 million contract, away in order to clear up salary cap space. Which team took Foles and his major monetary commitment off of Jacksonville's hands?

    a. Kansas City Chiefs
    b. Philadelphia Eagles
    c. St. Louis Rams
    d. Chicago Bears

10. In which Hawaiian city were Jaguars linemen on both sides of the ball (guard Vince Manuwai and end Tyson Alualu) born?

    a. Waikiki
    b. Maui
    c. Honolulu
    d. Hilo

11. Two players were teammates in college with the UCLA Bruins before taking the field together in Jacksonville as well. Which two players were they?

a. Quarterback Mark Brunell and defensive end Rob Meier

b. Kicker Josh Scobee and fullback Greg Jones

c. Guard Uche Nwaneri and defensive tackle Marcus Stroud

d. Running back Maurice Jones-Drew and tight end Marcedes Lewis

12. Jacksonville has never in its history completed a trade with any franchise in the NFC South division.

a. True

b. False

13. In 2020, the Jaguars traded star defensive end Yannick Ngakoue to the Minnesota Vikings. Which of the following creative conditions was placed on the fifth round draft choice that they received in return?

a. It turned into a 6th round pick if Ngakoue did not play at least 50% of the Vikings' defensive snaps

b. It turned into a 4th round pick if Ngakoue recorded 10 or more sacks the following season

c. It turned into a 3rd round pick if Ngakoue made the Pro Bowl and the Vikings won the Super Bowl

d. It turned into a 1st round pick if Ngakoue won the NFL's Defensive Player of the Year Award

14. In 2011, the Jaguars drafted guard Will Rackley, who played for Lehigh University, in the third round. What was his college team's nickname?

a. Mountain Hawks
b. Black Hawks
c. Red Hawks
d. Sky Hawks

15. Which of the following facts about Jaguars linebacker Paul Posluszny's tenure at Penn State University is NOT true?

    a. He was the first junior to be named a team captain for the Nittany Lions in nearly 40 years
    b. He was both a two time All-American and a two time Academic All American while at Penn State
    c. He won the Chuck Bednarik Award as the best defensive player in the nation two seasons in a row, becoming just the second player ever to do so
    d. He won the prestigious Draddy Trophy as the best student-athlete in the country

16. In their entire history, the Jaguars have never traded away a player who was born in the state of Florida.

    a. True
    b. False

17. Which prestigious Ivy League college program is the only one that the Jaguars have dipped into during the NFL Draft, selecting defensive tackle Seth Payne from the school in 1997?

    a. Harvard University
    b. Princeton University

c. Cornell University

d. Yale University

18. From which rival team did the Jaguars poach star offensive tackle Leon Searcy as a free agent in 1996?

a. San Diego Chargers

b. New England Patriots

c. Kansas City Chiefs

d. Pittsburgh Steelers

19. The talented and flamboyant Gardner Minshew II was a quarterback for which college squad before his time on the field with the Jaguars?

a. Washington State Cougars

b. New Mexico Lobos

c. Arizona State Sun Devils

d. Utah Utes

20. Jacksonville has completed more trades with the Cincinnati Bengals than with any other NFL franchise.

a. True

b. False

QUIZ ANSWERS

1. A – Detroit, Michigan

2. A – True

3. D – California

4. A – Center Brad Meester

5. B – Buffalo Bills

6. C – Delaware Tech Devils

7. B – False

8. A – Quarterback Blaine Gabbert

9. D – Chicago Bears

10. C – Honolulu

11. D – Running back Maurice Jones-Drew and tight end Marcedes Lewis

12. B – False

13. C – It turned into a 3rd round pick if Ngakoue made the Pro Bowl and the Vikings won the Super Bowl

14. A – Mountain Hawks

15. D – He won the prestigious Draddy Trophy as the best student-athlete in the country

16. B – False

17. C – Cornell University

18. D – Pittsburgh Steelers

19. A – Washington State Cougars

20. B – False

DID YOU KNOW?

1. When the Jaguars needed to trade quarterback Rob Johnson away from Jacksonville in 1998, the franchise sent him to Buffalo Bills in order to get the draft picks that they wanted. One of those draft picks became iconic Jaguars running back Fred Taylor, making the deal a big win for Jacksonville.

2. Jaguars linebacker Justin Durant beat the odds to be drafted into the NFL. Durant played at Hampton University, a school that does not traditionally receive much attention from NFL teams, but was good enough to be chosen in the second round in 2007 and went on to play for a decade in the NFL (though not all in Jacksonville).

3. The Jaguars and Tennessee Titans have had a fairly heated rivalry throughout their existence, particularly during the 1990's and 2000's. The two teams set aside their dislike for each other to make a small trade in 2020, in which Jacksonville obtained linebacker Kamalei Correa and a seventh round draft pick in exchange for giving up a sixth round draft pick.

4. At Maurice Jones-Drew's alma mater, UCLA, the future Jacksonville running back once left a game in progress when his college coach alerted MJD that his grandfather had had a heart attack while watching Jones-Drew break

93

off a 42 yard run in the third quarter. Sadly, his grandfather passed away.

5. One of the best free agent signings made by the Jaguars occurred heading into their second season, 1996, when they signed wide receiver Keenan McCardell away from the Cleveland Browns. McCardell was worth every penny as he formed a stalwart receiving tandem with Jimmy Smith that is still recognized as the best in Jacksonville history.

6. In a decision that was very popular at the time, Jacksonville signed free agent tight end Julius Thomas to a five-year contract worth $46 million to lure the Pro Bowler away from the Denver Broncos in 2015. Sadly, Thomas did not perform to that level with the Jaguars, was put on injured reserve during his second season with the club and was ultimately dealt to the Miami Dolphins as a failed experiment.

7. One of the larger and more impactful trades ever made by the Jaguars was completed October 15, 2019 with the Los Angeles Rams. Jacksonville sent All-Pro cornerback Jalen Ramsey to Los Angeles as he wanted to leave the team, and received three draft choices, including two first rounders, in the blockbuster. Ramsey would go on to become the highest-paid defensive back in this history of the NFL with the Rams, while the Jaguars used their new draft picks on running back Travis Etienne, and defensive ends K'Lavon Chiasson and Jordan Smith.

8. Fan favorite quarterback Mark Brunell was a part of Jacksonville's first ever NFL trade. As an expansion team in 1995, the Jaguars sent third- and fifth-round picks to the Green Bay Packers on April 21, 1995 to obtain Brunell, who remained with the team through 2003.

9. Defensive tackle Anthony Maddox remains the only Delta State Statesman ever taken by the Jaguars in an NFL draft. Maddox went 118th overall in the fourth round of the 2004 draft; the highest of the three players ever selected by an NFL team from that school.

10. Jacksonville hit the jackpot when they selected defensive end Rob Meier in the 2000 NFL Draft. Meier went 241st overall in the seventh round, which is not a range of the draft where many players succeed, but Meier played nine seasons for the Jaguars as a valuable rotation piece on their defensive line.

CHAPTER 10:

IN THE DRAFT ROOM

QUIZ TIME!

1. First ever Jaguars draft choice, left tackle Tony Boselli, attended USC, where he played for the football team that went by which nickname?

    a. Wildcats
    b. Trojans
    c. Eagles
    d. Golden Bears

2. For four consecutive years in the 2000's, the Jaguars traded out of the first round of the NFL draft, acquiring more proven talent in an effort to compete with the New England Patriots.

    a. True
    b. False

3. From which of these Texas-based college football programs have the Jaguars drafted the most players?

    a. Texas Longhorns
    b. Texas Tech Red Riders

c. Texas A&M Aggies

d. Texas El Paso Miners

4. During the first round of the 2020 NFL Draft, Jacksonville congratulated which of the following players on becoming a Jaguars remotely, via webcam, because of the COVID-19 pandemic that prevented the usual handshakes on stage?

a. Wide receiver Laviska Shenault of the Colorado Buffaloes

b. Linebacker Josh Allen of the Kentucky Wildcats

c. Cornerback C.J. Henderson of the Florida Gators

d. Offensive tackle Jawaan Taylor of the Florida Gators

5. The Jaguars selected two teammates from the Clemson Tigers offense in the first round of the 2021 NFL draft. Which teammates did they choose with the first and 25th picks?

a. Quarterback Trevor Lawrence and running back Travis Etienne

b. Wide receiver Laviska Shenault Jr. and offensive tackle Jawaan Taylor

c. Wide receiver D.J. Chark and running back Leonard Fournette

d. Wide receiver Allen Hurns and running back James Robinson

6. How many times in history has Jacksonville used a top 10 overall draft pick?

a. 8 times

b. 11 times

c. 15 times

d. 19 times

7. The Jaguars had never held the first overall pick in the NFL draft in the entire history of the franchise, before 2021.

   a. True

   b. False

8. Linebacker Josh Allen was drafted by the Jaguars in the first round in 2019 out of which school that is better known as a basketball powerhouse than a football school?

   a. Duke University

   b. University of North Carolina

   c. University of Kentucky

   d. Gonzaga University

9. Star linebacker Kevin Hardy was drafted by Jacksonville second overall in the 1996 NFL draft. Which excellent player was selected ahead of him?

   a. Defensive end Simeon Rice of the Arizona Cardinals

   b. Offensive tackle Jonathan Ogden of the Baltimore Ravens

   c. Offensive tackle Orlando Pace of St. Louis Rams

   d. Wide receiver Keyshawn Johnson of the New York Jets

10. After the 2021 NFL Draft had been completed, some of the grades that Jacksonville had given to college prospects became public knowledge. How did this unusual information come to light for football fans?

a. Mike Barnett, a scout who had been let go by the team days after the draft, posted the grades on Twitter in anger

b. In an episode of the Jaguars-produce series "The Hunt", the team forgot to blur out a draft board that was shown in one of the scenes

c. Jaguars general manager Trent Baalke released the grades to prove the validity of a comment he had made that he "couldn't believe (RB) Travis (Etienne) was still there for us at 25th overall"

d. An unknown computer hacker managed to break into the team's systems and anonymously posted draft grades, scouting reports, playbook details and other damaging information

11. What is the highest spot that Jacksonville has ever taken a specialist in the NFL draft, which they set by selecting punter Bryan Anger in 2012?

a. 1st round, 6th overall

b. 2nd round, 39th overall

c. 3rd round, 70th overall

d. 7th round, 224th overall

12. Perhaps due in part to their longstanding rivalry with the Tennessee Titans, Jacksonville has never drafted a player from the NCAA's Tennessee Volunteers.

a. True

b. False

13. Which draft choices did the Jaguars give up to the Baltimore Ravens in order to move up and select talented but injured linebacker Myles Jack with the 36th pick in the 2016 NFL Draft?

    a. The 53rd, 79th, and 186th overall selections
    b. The 60th, 88th, 107th, and 212th overall selections
    c. The 38th and 146th overall selections
    d. The 43rd and 128th overall selections

14. Defensive end Renaldo Wynn played four years of college ball for which program before being drafted by the Jaguars?

    a. Notre Dame Fighting Irish
    b. Texas Tech Red Raiders
    c. Cal State Fullerton Titans
    d. Ohio State Buckeyes

15. The Jaguars drafted two players from the Florida Gators who would go on to play more than 150 NFL games each. Who were these players?

    a. Defensive end Bobby McCray and linebacker Dante Fowler
    b. Linebacker Daryl Smith and center Brad Meester
    c. Defensive end Derrick Harvey and defensive tackle Taven Bryan
    d. Defensive back Reggie Nelson and running back Fred Taylor

16. Jaguars linebacker Myles Jack was such a talented athlete coming out of college that he was drafted in not one but three sports (basketball, baseball, and football).

    a. True
    b. False

17. When the Jaguars received the top choice in the 1995 NFL Expansion Draft, who did they select with it as the first cornerstone for their franchise?

    a. Quarterback Steve Beuerlein from the Arizona Cardinals
    b. Cornerback Corey Raymond from the New York Giants
    c. Cornerback Dave Thomas from the Dallas Cowboys
    d. Wide receiver Desmond Howard from the Washington Redskins

18. Between 2016-2020, Jacksonville selected a total of four quarterbacks in the sixth round of the NFL Draft in an attempt to lock down the position. Which of the four went lowest, at 203rd overall?

    a. Brandon Allen from the Arkansas Razorbacks
    b. Gardner Minshew II from the Washington State Cougars
    c. Tanner Lee from the Nebraska Cornhuskers
    d. Jake Luton from the Oregon State Beavers

19. Who did the Jacksonville Jaguars select with their two first round draft picks in the 1998 NFL Draft?

a. Florida running back Fred Taylor and Syracuse defensive back Donovin Darius

b. Illinois linebacker Kevin Hardy and Alabama defensive back Fernando Bryant

c. USC offensive tackle Tony Boselli and Tennessee running back James Stewart

d. Georgia Tech linebacker Keith Brooking and Oklahoma State defensive back R.W. McQuarters

20. From their first draft in 1995 until 2010, Jacksonville enjoyed a stretch in which they selected at least one player per year who lasted 100 games in the NFL.

a. True

b. False

QUIZ ANSWERS

1. B – Trojans

2. B – False

3. A – Texas Longhorns

4. C – Cornerback C.J. Henderson of the Florida Gators

5. A – Quarterback Trevor Lawrence and running back Travis Etienne

6. D – 19 times

7. A – True

8. C – University of Kentucky

9. D – Wide receiver Keyshawn Johnson of the New York Jets

10. B – In an episode of the Jaguars-produce series "The Hunt", the team forgot to blur out a draft board that was shown in one of the scenes

11. C – 3rd round, 70th overall

12. B – False

13. C – The 38th and 146th overall selections

14. A – Notre Dame Fighting Irish

15. D – Defensive back Reggie Nelson and running back Fred Taylor

16. B – False

17. A – Quarterback Steve Beuerlein from the Arizona Cardinals

18. C – Tanner Lee from the Nebraska Cornhuskers

19. A – Florida running back Fred Taylor and Syracuse defensive back Donovin Darius

20. A – True

DID YOU KNOW?

1. Quarterback Blake Bortles and linebacker Dante Fowler, who were both chosen third overall (Bortles in 2014, Fowler in 2015), are the highest drafted players the Jaguars have ever selected from colleges in their home state of Florida. Bortles went to Central Florida and Fowler was a Florida Gator.

2. The most players Jacksonville has drafted from any school is 12. This mark is held by the University of Florida, which may be the case due to simple local scouting opportunities, popularity with local fans, or simply coincidence.

3. Of the draft spots in the top ten in the NFL draft, Jacksonville has selected at 9th overall more than any other, choosing four players in that position. All have been successful in the NFL, but the best among them was probably franchise running back Fred Taylor.

4. Outside the top 10, Jacksonville has held the 39th, 159th and 180th overall picks four times apiece; more than any other spots in the draft. Their best choices from these vantage points include players at each level of the defense: defensive end Chris Smith, linebacker Daryl Smith and defensive back Rashean Mathis.

5. The Jaguars have never drafted a player from Jacksonville University, the University of North Florida, or Edward

Waters College, which are the three schools closest to the city.

6. Jacksonville has drafted precisely four players who have played a single game in the NFL. Three of them had their shining moment with the Jaguars, and one, fullback Marquez Williams, had his day on the field with the Cleveland Browns.

7. In the 2011 NFL Draft, Jacksonville selected quarterback Blaine Gabbert 10th overall, passing on quarterback Christian Ponder. who went two picks later to the Minnesota Vikings. The Jaguars could also have had the steady Andy Dalton or the explosive but controversial Colin Kaepernick, who were selected in the second round by the Cincinnati Bengals and San Francisco 49ers, respectively.

8. The smallest ever draft classes selected by the Jaguars in the NFL entry draft came in 2008 and 2011 when they took just five players each year. In both cases, the Jaguars were short on picks after trading up in the first round for a player they liked, and in 2008 Jacksonville traded up in the second round as well.

9. The largest Jaguars draft class ever was selected in 2020, when the team drafted a dozen players over the course of the draft. The selections were spread throughout the team's various needs, but did focus on improving the secondary, as four defensive backs were taken including cornerback C.J. Henderson in the first round.

10. The latest pick the Jaguars have made in the NFL draft was wide receiver Tiquan Underwood from Rutgers University, who the team chose 253rd overall in 2009. Despite the low selections and poor odds of it working out, Underwood did have modest success in the NFL. He stayed for two seasons with Jacksonville, getting into 13 games and making a handful of catches. His career continued with both the New England Patriots and Tampa Bay Buccaneers where he saw even more action, before ending in 2013 with over 1000 career receiving yards.

CHAPTER 11:

COACHES, GMS, & OWNERS

QUIZ TIME!

1. Who served as the Jaguars' first general manager?

    a. Michael Huyghue
    b. James Harris
    c. Tom Coughlin
    d. Wayne Weaver

2. Jacksonville general manager Tom Coughlin once proposed a deal to the New England Patriots that would have sent Jaguars icon Mark Brunell to Massachusetts in exchange for a young and then little-known Tom Brady.

    a. True
    b. False

3. The Jaguars' first head coach, Tom Coughlin, lasted for how long in that position with the franchise?

    a. One year
    b. Three years
    c. Eight years
    d. Twelve years

4. The Jaguars' most recent coach, Urban Meyer, rose through the coaching ranks to lead which NCAA programs before joining Jacksonville?

   a. UCLA, Oregon and Texas Tech
   b. Providence, Marshall, Virginia Tech and Clemson
   c. Washington State, Florida State and Nebraska
   d. Bowling Green, Utah, Florida and Ohio State

5. Who has owned the Jacksonville Jaguars for the longest amount of time?

   a. Wayne Weaver
   b. Shahid Khan
   c. Wayne Huizenga
   d. Stan Kroenke

6. Of all the Jacksonville bench bosses who have coached over 50 NFL games with the team, which one had the lowest winning percentage at only .226?

   a. Mike Mularkey
   b. Doug Marrone
   c. Jack Del Rio
   d. Gus Bradley

7. Jacksonville is the only NFL franchise to have a player rise from competing on the field for the team to ownership of the team.

   a. True
   b. False

8. Which coach led the Jaguars to their first division championship?

a. Tom Coughlin
b. Doug Marrone
c. Jack Del Rio
d. Gus Bradley

9. In 2011, the Jaguars employed the only interim head coach in the team's history who did not get hired to the role full time afterwards. Which coach led the team during this short five game span?

a. Running backs coach Earnest Byner
b. Defensive coordinator Mel Tucker
c. General manager Gene Smith
d. Offensive coordinator Dirk Koetter

10. Which unusual tactic did head coach Tom Coughlin employ to maintain order among the team's players?

a. Requiring that players sign in and out of the weight room so that the team would have a log of how often and for how long each player worked out
b. Dividing the team's cafeteria into two separate kitchens; one for skill players who needed healthy food to stay fit and one for linemen who needed large portions to maintain their bulk
c. Setting all of the facility's clocks ahead by 5-15 minutes so that everyone would be early for meetings
d. Closing the team's lounge area, which featured numerous table and video games for relaxation, during the week after a loss

11. The shortest ownership term for a Jacksonville Jaguars owner is held by Shahid Khan. For how long has he owned the team?

   a. Two years
   b. Four years
   c. Seven years
   d. Ten years

12. Coach Tom Coughlin's 1999 season is the benchmark in terms of winning percentage, as he led the team to a .875 winning percentage in the regular season.

   a. True
   b. False

13. Excluding current coach Urban Meyer, how many of the Jaguars' non-interim head coaches have spent their entire NFL coaching career (as of 2021) with Jacksonville?

   a. No head coaches
   b. One head coach
   c. Two head coaches
   d. Three head coaches

14. Which Jaguars general manager has led the franchise to the most playoff appearances?

   a. James Harris
   b. Tom Coughlin
   c. David Caldwell
   d. Gene Smith

15. Out of eight seasons coaching the Jaguars, how many times did coach Tom Coughlin finish above .500?

    a. Two seasons
    b. Four seasons
    c. Six seasons
    d. Seven seasons

16. At one point in their history, the Jaguars employed four coaches over a decade who had all started for Jacksonville at some point during their playing careers.

    a. True
    b. False

17. How did Shahid Khan become the majority owner of the Jacksonville Jaguars in 2011?

    a. He purchased the team when the previous owners wished to sell
    b. He inherited the team from his father
    c. He forced a takeover of the corporation that had previously owned the team
    d. He was hired as CEO of the company that owned the team

18. How many head coaches have roamed the sidelines for the Jaguars in their history?

    a. Three head coaches
    b. Five head coaches
    c. Six head coaches
    d. Fourteen head coaches

19. Which Jaguars coach is the only one to have won the United Press International award as the league's top coach, while behind the bench for Jacksonville?

    a. Doug Marrone
    b. Jack Del Rio
    c. Gus Bradley
    d. Tom Coughlin

20. Jaguars owner Shahid Khan once proposed trading franchises with New York Yankees owner George Steinbrenner, as part of a business deal.

    a. True
    b. False

QUIZ ANSWERS

1. C – Tom Coughlin

2. B – False

3. C – Eight years

4. D – Bowling Green, Utah, Florida and Ohio State

5. A – Wayne Weaver

6. D – Gus Bradley

7. B – False

8. A – Tom Coughlin

9. B – Defensive coordinator Mel Tucker

10. C – Setting all of the facility's clocks ahead by 5-15 minutes so that everyone would be early for meetings

11. D – Ten years

12. A – True

13. B – One head coaches

14. B – Tom Coughlin

15. B – Four seasons

16. B – False

17. A – He purchased the team when the previous owners wished to sell

18. C – Six head coaches

19. D – Tom Coughlin

20. B – False

DID YOU KNOW?

1. Only twice in team history have the Jaguars fired a coach midway through a season. The most recent occurred when Gus Bradley was 2-12 during his fourth season with the club when he was let go and replaced with Doug Marrone, who finished out the year 1-1.

2. Only one man has served as both coach and general manager of the Jaguars. Tom Coughlin was hired at the inception of the franchise to establish the team's culture and was in charge of both roles during his tenure.

3. Jacksonville owner Shahid Khan has invested in other sports as well. Khan bought English soccer team Fulham F.C. and is also the major investor in All Elite Wrestling. Luckily Khan's estimated $8 billion fortune allows him to devote more than adequate resources to each, as Khan is considered the 183rd richest human alive.

4. The Jaguars' original general manager, Tom Coughlin, lasted eight seasons in that role before Jacksonville finally made its first change.

5. Jaguars owner Shahid Khan purchased the franchise in 2012, and in so doing he became the first ever ethnic minority owner of an NFL organization.

6. Head coaches Tom Coughlin and Jack Del Rio spent very similar tenures with Jacksonville. The coaches are tied

atop the Jaguars' leaderboard with the highest number of regular season wins (68). Del Rio has more losses (71-60) though, along with a worse playoff record (1-2 and 4-4).

7. Only one Jaguars head coach has a winning record in the playoffs with Jacksonville. Doug Marrone went to 2-1 in the 2017 playoffs to finish his time with the team above .500.

8. The Jaguars have never had a head coach who was born outside the United States. They have employed just one head coach born in Florida, which was the home state of Mike Mularkey.

9. Jacksonville owner Shahid Khan was born in Lahore, Pakistan. Khan is one of just three NFL owners born in foreign countries, along with German Zygi Wilf of the Minnesota Vikings and South Korean Kim Pegula of the Buffalo Bills.

10. Never in league history has a Jacksonville general manager been awarded the Sporting News NFL Executive of the Year Award.

CHAPTER 12:

ODDS & ENDS

QUIZ TIME!

1. Which Jaguar has won the most Associated Press NFL MVP trophies while playing for Jacksonville?

   a. Running back Maurice Jones-Drew

   b. Quarterback Mark Brunell

   c. Wide receiver Jimmy Smith

   d. No Jaguar has ever been awarded this trophy

2. The first Jaguar to win any major award given out by the NFL was franchise defensive end Calais Campbell.

   a. True

   b. False

3. During which season did the Jaguars win their first Vince Lombardi Trophy as Super Bowl champions?

   a. 1999

   b. 2006

   c. 2018

   d. The Jaguars have never won a Super Bowl

4. In 2019, the NFL announced its All-Time Team, recognizing the 100 greatest players from the first 100 years of NFL history. How many of these players suited up for the Jaguars?

   a. 0 on offense, 0 on defense, and 0 on special teams
   b. 2 on offense, 1 on defense, and 0 on special teams
   c. 3 on offense, 3 on defense, and 1 on special teams
   d. 1 on offense, 4 on defense, and 0 on special teams

5. How many times has a Jacksonville Jaguar persevered through a negative event before returning to win the Comeback Player of the Year Award?

   a. Zero times
   b. One time
   c. Two times
   d. Four times

6. What is Frank Frangie's connection to the Jacksonville Jaguars?

   a. An architect who designed and built TIAA Bank Field for the Jaguars
   b. A beloved groundskeeper who has worked for the Jaguars since their inception
   c. A player agent who represented Mark Brunell, Maurice Jones-Drew, and several others
   d. A radio play by play announcer for the Jaguars on their home station

7. The Jacksonville Jaguars have the most wins of any franchise in NFL history.

a. True

b. False

8. Jacksonville is one of just four current NFL franchises that have never played in a Super Bowl. Which of the following teams is NOT in that group with the Jaguars?

a. Houston Texans

b. Cincinnati Bengals

c. Detroit Lions

d. Cleveland Browns

9. How many times has a Jaguars player won the NFL's Defensive Player of the Year Award.

a. Zero times

b. Two times

c. Three times

d. Five times

10. Which team has faced off five times against the Jaguars in the playoffs; more than any other NFL squad?

a. Buffalo Bills

b. Pittsburgh Steelers

c. New England Patriots

d. Denver Broncos

11. Jacksonville's TIAA Bank Field was the home of the world's largest what for nearly a decade?

a. Stadium pools (25 feet by 12 feet)

b. Locker rooms (200 feet by 65 feet)

c. Video boards (60 feet by 362 feet)

d. Jaguar statue (20 feet by 7 feet)

12. Jacksonville is the only NFL team to never appear in a Super Bowl despite hosting one.

    a. True
    b. False

13. Although his average yards per punt was 43.5, Jaguars punter Bryan Barker set the Jacksonville record for longest punt in franchise history by dropping one that traveled how far?

    a. 62 yards
    b. 68 yards
    c. 76 yards
    d. 83 yards

14. Kickers Josh Scobee and Josh Lambo, are tied for the franchise record for the longest field goal made. How long were these record-setting kicks?

    a. 57 yards
    b. 59 yards
    c. 61 yards
    d. 63 yards

15. When the Jaguars entered the AFC as an expansion franchise in 1995, which other expansion team was placed in the NFC at the same time to balance out the number of teams?

    a. Tampa Bay Buccaneers
    b. Arizona Cardinals
    c. Carolina Panthers
    d. Atlanta Falcons

16. Kicker Josh Scobee has *missed* more field goals during his Jaguars career than any other Jacksonville player has even *attempted*.

    a. True
    b. False

17. Which Jaguars kicker (with at least 50 kicks attempted), holds the team's highest field goal percentage, at an excellent 95% made?

    a. Josh Lambo
    b. Jason Myers
    c. Mike Hollis
    d. Josh Scobee

18. What is the name of the Jacksonville Jaguars' "Hall of Fame" for their own players?

    a. The Jacksonville Ring of Honor
    b. The Great Wall of Jaguars
    c. The Pride of the Jaguars
    d. The Jacksonville Honor Society

19. Against which teams do the Jaguars have undefeated records in the NFL playoffs?

    a. Denver Broncos and Miami Dolphins
    b. Indianapolis Colts, Buffalo Bills, Tennessee Titans and New York Jets
    c. New England Patriots and Pittsburgh Steelers
    d. Buffalo Bills, Miami Dolphins and Pittsburgh Steelers

20. Although TIAA Bank Field's capacity is listed as 67,814 people, the Jaguars announced an attendance of 72,363 fans at their very first home game in 1995.

   a. True
   b. False

QUIZ ANSWERS

1. D – No Jaguar has ever been awarded this trophy

2. B – False

3. D – The Jaguars have never won a Super Bowl

4. A – 0 on offense, 0 on defense, and 0 on special teams

5. A – Zero times

6. D – A radio play by play announcer for the Jaguars on their home station

7. B – False

8. B – Cincinnati Bengals

9. A – Zero times

10. C – New England Patriots

11. C – Video boards (60 feet by 362 feet)

12. B – False

13. D – 83 yards

14. B – 59 yards

15. C – Carolina Panthers

16. B – False

17. A – Josh Lambo

18. C – The Pride of the Jaguars

19. D – Buffalo Bills, Miami Dolphins and Pittsburgh Steelers

20. A – True

DID YOU KNOW?

1. One Jaguar has won the NFL's Walter Payton Man of the Year Award. Defensive end Calais Campbell was honored with this distinction for the 2019 season.

2. After just their second year of existence, the Jaguars sent quarterback Mark Brunell to the Pro Bowl in Hawaii after the 1996 season where he won the Pro Bowl MVP Award.

3. Jaguars icons Keenan McCardell and Jimmy Smith were always an excellent pair in Jacksonville, so it's not much of a surprise that McCardell ranks 24th on the all-time list for most receptions in NFL history, while Jimmy Smith is right behind him in the 25th spot.

4. Although some NFL teams don't use them, Jacksonville has had a cheerleading squad since they began playing in 1995. The Jacksonville Roar appear at the team's games, are active at community events, and also put out a swimsuit calendar each year. There is also a Junior Roar group for kids who are interested in cheerleading.

5. The Jaguars' value is estimated at $2.45 billion by Forbes magazine, which ranks them as the 25th most valuable NFL team, right between the New Orleans Saints and Cleveland Browns.

6. Jaxson de Ville, the Jaguars mascot, is a yellow jaguar with teal accents who wears shorts, running shoes, sunglasses,

and a Jacksonville jersey with a paw print on the front. The mascot is a bit of a thrill seeker and sometimes enters the stadium by ziplining or bungee jumping in.

7. Jacksonville has a winning record against eight other current NFL teams. The Jaguars have gotten the better of the: Cleveland Browns, New York Giants, New York Jets, Tampa Bay Buccaneers, Cincinnati Bengals, Las Vegas Raiders, Baltimore Ravens and Denver Broncos.

8. The Jaguars have played more games against the Tennessee Titans than any other team in the NFL. The two clubs have faced off 52 times in the regular season, with the Indianapolis Colts a distant second at 40 total matchups.

9. Tony Khan, the son of Jaguars majority owner Shahid Khan, is listed as a co-owner of the franchise and currently serves in the capacity of Chief Football Strategy Officer.

10. The Jaguars have always been an excellent partner in the Jacksonville community. Upon becoming an NFL franchise, they immediately established the Jacksonville Jaguars Foundation, which to date has donated over $20 million to benefit local areas and dozens of charities.

CONCLUSION

There you have it; an amazing collection of Jaguars trivia, information, and statistics at your fingertips! Regardless of how you fared on the quizzes, we hope that you found this book entertaining, enlightening, and educational.

Ideally you knew many of these details, but also learned a good deal more about the history of the Jacksonville Jaguars, their players, coaches, management, and some of the quirky stories surrounding the team. If you got a little peek into the colorful details that make being a fan so much more enjoyable, then mission accomplished!

The good news is, the trivia doesn't have to stop there! Spread the word. Challenge your fellow Jaguars fans to see if they can do any better. Share some of the stories with the next generation to help them become Jacksonville supporters too.

If you are a big enough Jaguars fan, consider creating your own quiz with some of the details you know that weren't presented here, and then test your friends to see if they can match your knowledge.

The Jacksonville Jaguars might not be the most storied franchise, but they have had multiple periods of success mixed into the not-so-successful spells. They've had glorious superstars, iconic moments, hilarious tales ... but most of all they have wonderful, passionate fans. Thank you for being one of them.

Made in the USA
Las Vegas, NV
07 December 2021

36522411R00075